Jesus
and
Social Ethics

by

Stephen C. Mott

Professor of Christian Social Ethics at Gordon-Conwell Theological Seminary, South Hamilton, Mass., U.S.A.

GROVE BOOKS

BRAMCOTE **NOTTS.** **NG9 3DS**

CONTENTS

ACKNOWLEDGEMENT

This Booklet is an edited version of two articles on 'The Use of the New Testament in Social Ethics' which appeared in *Transformation* (an International Dialogue on Evangelical Social Ethics, published by the Theological Commission Unit on Ethics and Society of the World Evangelical Fellowship, Paternoster Press, 3 Mount Radford Crescent, Exeter)Vol. 1, nos. 2 and 3 (1984), and the material is reproduced here by permission which is gratefully acknowledged. In its original writing, and as reproduced here, it is intended to complement Grove Booklet on Ethics no. 51, Christopher J. H. Wright *The Use of the Bible in Social Ethics* (Grove Books, 1983), a study which specifically concentrates on the Old Testament.

THE COVER PICTURE

is by Greg Forster

First Impression October 1984

ISSN 0305–4241

ISBN 0 907536 78 6

INTRODUCTION: THE PROBLEM

The Bible as a social document is as closed to most biblical scholarship as if it had been written in a yet undeciphered language.[1]

Objections to using the New Testament for contemporary social ethics come from both ends of the theological spectrum. They have been raised by both biblical scholars and Christian ethicists. Denial of the legitimacy of this use of the New Testament takes three forms: 1 Denial of the social content of the New Testament; 2. denial that the New Testament is concerned with ethics; 3. denial that New Testament social thought is either available to us or practical for us today.

On the other hand, great numbers of Christians who have been involved in social change and social service consider the New Testament to be foundational to their activity. Great Christian social movements have drawn upon it. Have they been deceived about what has guided their behaviour and, in the process, misused the biblical documents?

When the breadth and diversity of its ethical thought is understood, the New Testament makes valid, significant and essential contributions to Christian social ethics.

1. THE SOCIAL CONTENT OF THE NEW TESTAMENT

a. The Detractors

Christians in the fundamentalist, liberal and existentialist traditions have argued that the New Testament does not provide instruction for the ordering of social relations, Without great difficulty one can picture portions of the chapter, 'the Limitations of Jesus' Social Teaching'[2], by the Harvard Quaker and New Testament scholar, Henry Cadbury, being reprinted in a fundamentalist magazine.

One common idea is that the New Testament reverses the Old Testament emphasis on community and justice. God's ways with humanity and internalized and spiritualized. Those who do not find the New Testament to be socially relevant may either lament or rejoice at this alleged change of direction. The nature of the teaching and activity of Jesus in his earthly life is particularly at stake.

Ernst Troeltsch presented Jesus as teaching a heroic religious and ethical individualism. Troeltsch is significant not only because he represents the interpretation of Jesus in German liberalism made formerly by such people as Adolf Harnack[3], but also because he greatly

---

[1] Norman K. Gottwald and Antoinette C. Wire, 'Introduction', to *The Bible and Liberation*, ed. Gottwald and Wire (Berkeley, CA, Community for Religous Research and Education, 1976), p.4. I regret that Thomas W. Ogletree's important work, *The Use of the Bible in Christian Ethics* (Fortress, Philadelphia), came out too late in 1983 for me to consult it.

[2] Henry J. Cadbury, *The Peril of Modernizing Jesus* (Macmillan, New York, 1937), ch.5.

[3] *cf.* Richard H. Hiers, *Jesus and Ethics, Four Interpretations* (Philadelphia: Westminster, 1968), pp.28, 35. The Kingdom of God for Harnack meant individual experience: 'God and the soul, the soul and its God'.

influenced later ethicists, such as Reinhold Niebuhr in their reading of Jesus. For the great philosopher and sociologist of religion, the ideal Jesus taught meant 'the entire renunciation of the material social ideal of all political and economic values, and the turning towards the religious treasures of peace of heart, love of humanity, fellowship with God, which are open to all because they are not subject to any difficulties of leadership or organization'.[1] Jesus offered no tangible of material reward but rather the Kingdom of God understood as a religious goal. Equity and justice, Troeltsch argued, were dealt with only casually by Jesus. Thus Jesus had no programme of social reform. He summoned people to prepare for the coming of the kingdom 'quietly within the framework of the present world-order, in a purely religious fellowship of love, with an earnest endeavour to conquer self and cultivate the Christian virtues'.[2]

Rudolf Bultmann and Henry Cadbury have argued that the focus on the individual and small group, rather than on social structures, was a necessary consequence of Jesus' thought. Bultmann held that apart from a teaching of love, which was without supporting ethical norms, Jesus did not teach a system of values: '. . . Jesus teaches no ethics at all in the sense of an intelligible theory valid for all men concerning what should be done and left undone'. That type of theory, Bultmann argued, would require a doctrine about human nature lacking in Jesus' teaching. Jesus presented human beings as insecure people. He did not have a concept of human nature which included personality, values, or particular abilities and goals for human endeavour.[3] Cadbury found that Jesus' alleged disinterest in social institutions derived from his simplified understanding of society and interpersonal relationships. Jesus' teaching lacks the essential ingredients necessary for a social ethic; a concept of the group and a recognition that others have rights or needs. Jesus, even in his teaching on wealth and charity, focused on the needs of the giver rather than the condition of the recipient.[4]

Such arguments for the New Testament's stress on the individual, in Jesus' teaching in particular, are defective because they do not provide a sufficient framework for the importance they place upon the individual and the church. Three crucial elements of New Testament thought, which provide a social framework for its teaching, are missing: the relationship of the New Testament to the Old Testament; the importance of status in social structures; and the concept of the cosmic 'principalities and powers'.

[1] Ernst Troeltsch, *The Social Teachings of the Christian Churches* (Harper, New York, 1960 [1911]), Vol. 1, pp.48-49.

[2] Troeltsch, p.61; *cf.* pp.53-54. For a modern ethicist who approves of Troeltsch's interpretation that Jesus' task was to prepare a Christian community with Christian virtues, *cf.* Stanley Hauerwas, 'Jesus: The Story of the Kingdom', in Hauerwas, *A Community of Character* (Notre Dame, Ind., U. of Notre Dame, 1981), pp.38-39. Hauerwas, however, rebukes Troeltsch for not seeing that an emphasis on parishes or families rather than on the empire is a social ethic.

[3] Rudolf Bultmann, *Jesus and the Word* (Scribner's New York, 1934), pp.84-85; *cf.* p.94; Hiers, *Jesus and Ethics*, p.86.

[4] Cadbury, *Peril*, pp.97, 102, 116.

4

b The Relationship between Old and New Testaments

One of the first comments to be made regarding the contribution of the New Testament to social ethics is that without the Old Testament, it is incomplete. Christopher Wright pointed out that Jesus is presented in the New Testament as servant, he is understood as the embodiment of Israel, the people of God. He has inherited and is passing on to the new messianic community the social role and intention of Old Testament Israel.[1] The Old Testament was the Scripture of Jesus and the early church. The statement of the later Pauline church that this Scripture was 'useful . . . for instruction in righteousness' (or 'education in justice' [paideia ten en diakaiosyne], 2 Tim. 3.16) was only articulating the assumption the church made from the beginning. Old Testament ethical principles accepted by these communities were not necessarily restated; they did not need to be, for they already were in Scripture. As a result New Testament ethical topics, raised to meet ad hoc problems, do not form the entire content of the New Testament church's ethical belief. In exegesis, one must be continually alert to the 'continuity of content' of which the Decalogue is only the most obvious example.[2] Behind the New Testament lies an authoritative text which demonstrates deep concern for the social order, for justice, for the economic and social relationships of the powerful and the weak.

New Testament writers have interpreted new life in Christ in continuity with the Old Testament's social hopes and concerns. Luke 1 and 2 are an essential introduction to the whole Gospel. Jesus came to and was received by humble people of the land who were looking for the manifestation of divine power to reverse the roles of possessors and the dispossessed by bringing in social and economic justice (Luke 1.52-53). These chapters, which are everywhere impregnated (Davies) with the notion of fulfilment, reflect the fact that Christians interpreted their experiences in light of their reading of the Old Testament, including its message of justice. The writer, by the way he constructs his Gospel, reveals his agreement with their perspective.[3] The positioning of the famous Nazareth sermon expresses a similar interpretation. Luke 4.18-21 provides the first presentation of Jesus' preaching. The passage serves as his inaugural sermon. The Old Testament text which is read identifies Jesus' mission as a comprehensive liberation understood in a Hebrew way. Likewise the Sermon on the Mount in Matthew is the first presentation of Jesus'

---

[1] Christopher J. H. Wright, *The Use of the Bible in Social Ethics* (Grove Booklets on Ethics 51, Bramcote, Notts., 1983), p.22.

[2] *Cf.* Brevard Childs, *Biblical Theology in Crisis* (Westminster, Philadelphia, 1970), p.128. Pp.123-38 treat 'Biblical Theology's Role in Decision-Making'. Childs notes that in interpretation the movement between the Testaments does not go in one direction only (p.113).

[3] W. D. Davies may be correct that in Luke 2.23 and Acts 1.8 Luke corrected a nationalistic fervour (*The Gospel and the Land. Early Christianity and Jewish Territorial Doctrine* [Berkeley, U. of California, 1974], pp.263-64). But Lukan themes also show his approval of the fulfilment of social justice separable from nationalism. Similarly, it might be noted that in this book, Davies deals with land as a national concept but not as means of production, possessed by families. This is a different concept which has its own biblical importance.

teaching. It too is an inaugural address. The Beatitudes which begin the Sermon deal with similar groups of afflicted people (the standard recipients of justice in the Old Testament). They connect Jesus to the Old Testament concern for justice for the weak. Finally, all the Gospels introduce Jesus' public ministry with that of John the Baptist. John the Baptist, who in Q is the greatest of the prophets (Matt. 11.9; Luke 7.26, cf. Mark 9.13), is presented in each of the Synoptic Gospels as a preacher of repentance in accordance with the Old Testament prophecy of social righteousness (Mark 1.3-4 par.). In Luke, John is related to the believing remnant of chapters 1 and 2. All the Gospel writers make John a prominent link between Jesus and the Old Testament social tradition.[1]

In addition to these important ways of structuring their Gospels, the authors reveal in other ways that they assume the Old Testament teaching on justice. In the Q material of Matthew 23.23 and Luke 11.42, Jesus demands justice of his hearers. Matthew identifies this justice as belonging to the more important part of the Law. In the story of Lazarus and Dives in Luke 16, Dives wants to send Lazarus back from the dead to warn his brothers that in a social reversal of fortunes those who keep their wealth from the poor are sent into torment. He is told that they have Moses and the prophets, who are sufficient (Luke 16.29-31). This story follows the statement: 'Heaven and earth can pass away more easily than one "dot" from the Law' (v.17). The Old Testament is both normative and adequate in its teachings about property relations. The Parable of the Wicked Husbandmen (Matt. 21.31-46; Mark 12.1-12; Luke 20.9-19) further connects Jesus to the prophetic tradition. Jesus, the son, has the same mission as the prophets of the Old Testament who are the slaves of the owner of the vineyard. All have the task of calling the leaders of the people, the farmers, to account for failing to produce the fruits of the vineyard. Matthew (21.43) states that the failure is one of not 'bearing the fruits' of the Reign of God.

Turning to another section of the New Testament, Luke Johnson has argued recently that Leviticus 19 guided several of the ethical injunctions in James: James quotes Leviticus 19.18 in James 2.8 ('you shall love your neighbour as yourself'). Furthermore, by applying this love command to the problem of partiality (James 2.1, 9), the author of James shows that he has read Leviticus 19.18 in context, since Leviticus 19.15 forbids partiality. The condemnation of holding back the wages of workers in James 5.4 reflects the prohibition recorded in Leviticus 19.13.

Noting other parallels, Johnson concludes that James regarded the royal law by which Christians are to live to be shown concretely and specifically not only in the Decalogue (2.11) but also in the commands

---

[1] This was Walter Rauschenbusch's perspective on John the Baptist. Cf. Allen Dale Verhay, 'The Use of Scripture in Moral Discourse: A Case Study of Walter Rauschenbusch' (Yale U. Ph.D. dissertation, 1975; Ann Arbor, MI, University Microfilms, 1978), p.99. A strength of Rauschenbusch's vigorous interpretation of Jesus' social teaching is that he places Jesus in continuity with the Old Testament prophetic tradition (cf. Verhay, pp.71, 97-99, 165).

found in Leviticus 19.12-18.[1] We find behind the epistle another Christian community which, in responding to issues facing it, reflected upon Old Testament ethical materials.

What does recognition of continuity with the Old Testament do for the study of New Testament ethics and particularly the ethics of Jesus? Bultmann and Cadbury argued that Jesus lacked both a concept of human nature and a social theory of rights and needs. When we only know about an individual of the past from a few written documents— Cadbury writes that all we have of Jesus are a few aphorisms, comments, or parables—it is not methodologically sound to argue from silence that that person lacks specific ideas. Anyone's thought should be interpreted in terms of that person's normative culture. For Jesus the Old Testament was an important component of his culture and supplied an anthropology and social perception said to be lacking. For example, groups in the Old Testament who are to be the recipients of justice, such as the sick, the poor, the stranger, and the widow, are identified by the particular form of their need. Members of these groups frequently appear in the Gospels. From this background one perceives that Jesus intentionally responded not merely to individuals but also to groups. His response reflected both his recognition of specific human needs and the corresponding claims they pose upon the community. To identify such classes of victims presupposes some perception of the social organism which exploits or excludes them.

The Old Testament is also needed to understand more fully the first person of the Godhead. God the Redeemer is recognized also as Creator; God's saving concerns include the whole creation, and God is concerned with the morality of the social orders and not merely with the salvation of individuals or small groups of individuals. It is this perspective which is lacking in attempts to interpret the words of the sermon in Nazareth or the Beatitudes as metaphors for ideas about salvation and existence interpreted only in terms of individuals.

When Jesus' social tradition is recognized, the concept of justice, rooted in the Old Testament, can be identified.[2] This is a justice oriented toward the distribution of goods to meet basic needs and in particular to secure that which is essential for minimal participation in the community. Accordingly, it is a particular justice because need is particular. It often requires taking the side of the poor against what has been advantageous to the rich. The Lukan form of the Beatitudes with its contrast between blessings on the poor and woes on the rich is a graphic expression of this conception of justice.

Acknowledging this background would prevent some basic misunderstandings of Jesus' ethic. Reinhold Niebuhr, in the tradition of Troeltsch, understood Jesus to have taught a noble, perfectionist standard of pure love. He argued that, in assuming the responsibilities

[1] Luke T. Johnson, 'The Use of Leviticus 19 in the Letter of James', *Journal of Biblical Literature* 101 (1982), 391-401.
[2] For development of this concept of justice, please see chapter 4 of my book, *Biblical Ethics and Social Change* (Oxford U., New York, 1982).

of our societies, we must make choices and distinctions not provided by this pure ethic of love. We need a fragment of justice not taught by Jesus, Niebuhr stated, that asserts the rights of the disinherited and makes a choice between privilege and need. It is a justice which is imaginative in gauging the needs of those who suffer from social injustice.[1] Reinhold's brother, H. Richard, corrected him. Jesus did not teach a virtue of love which stood by itself apart from all other virtues. Rather, Jesus taught love as being disproportionate among allegiances in its devotion to the one God. He did not mean that it was unaccompanied by other virtues perhaps equally as great.[2] These virtues include the Old Testament's view of justice which is close to the justice that Reinhold Niebuhr describes—the discriminating justice which sides with the downtrodden, as in Mary's Magnificat, the Nazareth sermon, the Beatitudes, and the Parables.[3]

When Cadbury writes that in the parable of the workers in the vineyard Jesus flouts the idea of a uniformly applicable principle, he is thinking of the liberal view of justice not that of the tradition in which Jesus stood.[4] Troeltsch likewise misunderstands Jesus' commitment to justice when he interprets Jesus' bias to the poor as 'the privilege of suffering for the sake of the knowledge of God and of the true values of life'. The socially partial texts in the New Testament, such as passages in Luke which may glorify poverty and in James which attack the rich, Troeltsch attributes to 'the spirit of people with a narrow outlook', 'the spirit of small minds'. He sets aside the passages in Luke dealing with poverty and wealth as 'Ebionite'.[5] Those who dismiss the social relevance of Jesus tend to neglect or disregard the Lukan themes dealing with the needy and property.[6]

A most significant consequence of interpreting New Testament ethics in continuity with the Old Testament is the impact it makes upon the concept of the reign of God.[7] God's reign sums up the hope of the Old Testament. It speaks of God's intervention in history to produce a new age in which there would not be a new relationship of faith and obedience to God but a new social order. The coming of this new rule of God is that salvation in which God's creation is renewed in such a way that creation and redemption become merged.

[1] Reinhold Neibuhr, 'The Ethic of Jesus and the Social Problem' (1932), in Niebuhr, Love and Justice, ed. D. B. Robertson (Smith, Gloucester, MA, 1957), pp.32-33, 34, 37, 40.
[2] H. Richard Niebuhr, Christ and Culture (Harper, New York, 1951), p.16. The whole section, 'Toward a Definition of Christ' (pp.11-29), is relevant.
[3] As Heinz Schümann notes, through the early Christian apostles, prophets, and teachers the love command in Jesus' teaching becomes sharply and socially critical in the context of threats against the rich and the established and partisanship for the poor and the weak ('Das eschatologische Heil Gottes und Die Weltverantwortung des Menschen', Geist und Leben 50 [1977], 28).
[4] Cadbury, Peril, p.100.
[5] Troeltsch, Social Teachings, Vol. 1, pp.60, 161, 170-1.
[6] Another example is Jack T. Sanders, Ethics in the New Testament (Fortress, Philadelphia, 1975), p.36.
[7] For the development of the concept of the Reign of God, cf. Mott, Biblical Ethics, Xh,5.

In the New Testament the Reign of God formed a major part of Jesus' teaching. In Pauline thought it linked with Christ's conquest of the cosmic powers (1 Cor. 15.24). Beyond the actual use of the term *(basileia)*, recovery of God's sovereign rule over all things is present in the liberation of creation in Romans 8 and in the reconciliation of all things in Colossians and Ephesians.

The Reign provides a context for God's universal ethical concerns. It also furnishes a concept of history into which other New Testament themes can be placed. We understand that Jesus in his ethics was proclaiming a new social order breaking into history in his ministry. Satan's hold on the created world crumbles: he is bound and his goods are plundered (Matt. 12.28-29; Luke 11.20-22).

This understanding of the reign of God in the Gospels is not universally accepted. It is denied by many who question the New Testament's relevance to social ethics. A logical progression can be traced from a neglect of the Old Testament context for New Testament ethics to a denial of the social aspects of the Reign of God to a dismissal of the social ethics of the New Testament. Harry Cadbury was not sure what was the appropriate background for the term, Kingdom of God. He stated that there was no evidence that Jesus used it with social connotations.[1] Stanley Hauerwas denies that ethical norms are connected to the Kingdom of God because Jesus is the Kingdom in person.[2] The difficulty with this commonly held position is that the Synoptic Gospels present Jesus as one who proclaims and is an agent of the Reign but who directs little attention to his own being. From the perspective of the whole of the New Testament, we understand that Jesus as the incarnation of God inaugurates and empowers God's new Reign through his life, death, and resurrection. But he is not that Reign. The Reign is the sphere where he conquers those powers which are destructive of the creation. When their defeat is accomplished at his coming again, he hands the Reign over to God (1 Cor. 15.24-28).

The social meaning of the Reign of God is also obscured when it is defined as a symbol. *Symbol* is used by Bultmann and Paul Tillich in contrast to a *concept:* one invokes an experience of power or authenticity, the other contains its own truth claim. According to an existential interpretation, the Reign does not denote a good rule, a new social order, as if it were a concept. Rather, it discloses God's presence and availability in the world to the individual, demanding an urgent response of obedience and the abandonment of false securities. An extreme example of this reinterpretation is the way Jack Sanders and John Crossan expound the Good Samaritan. Crossan argues that the questions asked before and after the story, including the reference to the double commandment of love, are secondary to the parable. The story was not originally about love, as Luke presents it. Rather it is a metaphor about the coming of the Reign. The surprise of finding that

---

[1] Cadbury, *Peril,* p.94.
[2] Hauerwas, 'Jesus', pp.44-45.

the Samaritan is good leads one to see that the coming of the Kingdom breaks one's previous values and established conclusions about life.[1]

I would criticize this conclusion in terms of *Sachkritik* (a critical analysis of a passage in terms of its subject matter). The interpretation is based on a pre-understanding of Jesus' teaching. Yet this pre-understanding does not fully understand the Reign, for it has separated from both its biblical background and its social and ethical content. As Amos Wilder points out, the assumptions about human nature are so deficient because objective content has been removed from Jesus' teaching. The human being is seen primarily as one who wills and strives rather than as a cultural being endowed with intellect and imagination. It also ignores the dogma upon which Jesus' words rested.[2] In the light of a more substantial and enriched *Sachkritik* Luke's interpretation of the Good Samaritan in terms of love as a basic value of the new social order of God's Reign makes better sense.

There is also an Evangelical interpretation which treats the Reign as symbol. I. H. Marshall, for example, approves the view of Norman Perrin, from the existential school, that the Reign is a symbol rather than a concept. For Marshall the Reign does not refer to rule but to God bringing his people salvation. It can be restated without loss as the Gospel of free grace.[3] However, when understood in the light of the Old Testament background, the concept of rule includes salvation. The king's main function was to achieve deliverance (e.g. 1 Sam. 10.1). The majority of cases in the Old Testament which call God King refer to the deliverance God works. The concept of a just rule and an ideal order is part of the New Testament's portrayal of Reign. The best description occurs in the Lord's Prayer. 'Your Kingdom come, your will be done on earth as it is in Heaven'. The existential symbolic interpretation is not so much wrong in either its Bultmannian or Evangelical form, as deprived of the rich content of the Reign of God, including the universal, cosmic, and public scope of God's work and sovereignty.

The concept of the Reign of God presses us to deal with what is new in the New Testament in contrast to the social tradition it has inherited. Jesus is the fulfilment of as well as the guide to this tradition.[4] As fulfilment Jesus' death and resurrection are the central acts of the

---

[1] Sanders, *Ethics in the New Testament*, p.6; John Dominic Crossan, 'Parable and Example in the Teaching of Jesus', *New Testament Studies* 18 (1972), 295. Sanders goes beyond Crossan in criticizing him for allowing that the parable in the literal stage teaches an exemplary conduct. For Sanders the only meaning is the metaphorical point about the Kingdom. John C. Hoffman argues that Crossan in his exegesis is controlled by an epistemology which is agnostic concerning objective reality ('Story as Mythoparabolic Medium: Reflections on Crossan's Interpretation of the Parables', *Union Seminary Quarterly Review* 37 (1983), 323-33).

[2] Amos N. Wilder, 'The Word as Address and the Word as Meaning', in *New Frontiers in Theology. Vol.2: The New Hermeneutic*, ed. J. Robinson and J. Cobb (Harper, New York, 1964), pp.202,213.

[3] I. Howard Marshall, 'Preaching the Kingdom of God', *Expository Times* 89 (1977), 15.

[4] *Cf.* G. Ernest Wright, 'From the Bible to the Modern World', in *Biblical Authority for Today*, ed. A. Richardson and W. Schweitzer (Westminster, Philadelphia, 1951), p.228.

coming of the Reign. The Reign breaks into the lives of those who share in the new life in Christ, and into the world as the Gospel of grace through faith which bursts national boundaries. As a guide to the tradition, Jesus confirms the demands for the ordering of life already given and expected. He radicalizes them, and clarifies their true meaning.

The New Testament presents the arrival of a new moment in the tension between partial fulfilment and urgency about the end. A new way of life is occurring and is about to come. Its significance is seen when one considers parallels between Jesus and Jewish rabbis in their teaching on the poor. For example, the social reversal in the Parable of Dives and Lazarus can be compared to the Jewish maxim, 'The rich help the poor in this world, but the poor help the rich in the world to come'. Similarly, one can point to the similarities between the best thought of Judaism and the restitution made by Zacchaeus.[1] But for Jesus, these are not wisdom maxims or legal commentary for a basic society. Jesus' counsels are nothing other than the principles of conduct of God's Reign emerging in concrete form.[2] The raising of the poor and the reversal of wealth are part of a great social movement as God enters into history with blessings and fearful judgment. A new order is rivalling the old; we make our choice face to face with salvation and judgment.

c. The Place of Status in Society and in the Message of the New Testament

The second crucial factor in identifying the social content of the New Testament is the importance of status in its pages. In Old Testament social ethics economic deprivation is the central concern; in the New Testament status is the key to social ethics. Even when scholars have interpreted correctly the many passages which deal with status, they have frequently failed to identify adequately the sociological characteristics of status present or to realize the importance that status has for the social system. In general the Old Testament is concerned with class while the New Testament is concerned with status. There are, however, important overlaps.

The contrast between class and status is important and helpful for our purposes, although it is a simplification because there are many forms of each. Class deals with the economic opportunities that an individual can expect in life by virtue of the group to which he or she belongs. It is related to property relations and economic power. It is objective. Status is subjective. It is based on the value the culture places on various groups of people. On account of certain characteristics, prestige and respect (or its lack) are granted by custom or law. Material rewards and opportunities may be included with status or they may be its

---

[1] *Cf.* Frederick C. Grant, 'Method in Studying Jesus' Social Teaching', in *Studies in Early Christianity,* F. Porter and B. Wisner Fest., ed. S. Case (Century, New York, 1928), p.269.

[2] Hermet Merklein, as quoted by Rudolf Schnackenburg in 'Neutestamentliche Ethik im Kontext heutiger Wirklichkeit', in *Anspruch der Wirklichkeit und christlicher Glaube,* A. Auer Fest., ed. H. Weber and D. Mieth (Patmos, Dusseldorf, 1980), p.205.

consequence. What matters in receiving esteem or dishonour is not so much what you are as what people think you are. Both class (economic position) and status (social position) are power resources.[1] Jesus' teaching of universal love for those who belonged to the various groupings of his social world relates to status and forms a major segment of the New Testament ethic. Another major part of this ethic, which also involves status, is the concern in the Epistles over how the new Christian communities are to be formed and who is to be included.

The story of Zacchaeus (Luke 19.1-10) is a good basis for showing the importance of the question about status in Jesus' teaching. Verse 7 stands out because structurally it is in the centre of the meeting between Zacchaeus and Jesus (vv.5-10). It also stands in sharp contrast to Zacchaeus' joy and response to Jesus' action in seeking, receiving, and affirming him: 'Everyone grumbled, saying, "He has gone to lodge with a man who is a sinner".' The text states that 'everyone' joined in this evaluation of Zacchaeus. The whole community agreed that Zacchaeus was a 'sinner'. That was his status in society.

The term *sinner (hamartolos)* was not a moral description but a technical term. It was a title used to refer to a group of people who could be both identified and segregated. In the Gospels the 'sinners' are the tax collectors, prostitutes, and drunkards. They are characterized by an observable lifestyle or economic activity which has been ethically condemned. In the Hellenistic world a 'sinner' was the opposite of those who are right and proper ('our kind of people'). For Jewish writers it was a derogatory term of abuse[2]. No matter what other attributes Zacchaeus had, as a tax collector he was a 'sinner' and therefore cut off and despised.

Jesus was accused frequently of his intimate association with 'sinners' (in the Orient table fellowship signifies sharing an intimate community of life[3]). Why was he accused? Why was it a matter of such concern? Jesus, like Paul later, was crossing socially important boundaries. Status depends on separation and the avoidance of communications that imply acceptance and equality. Jesus by intentionally and habitually crossing those boundaries, showed how he defined status. Jesus' deliberate action is shown in his response to the accusation (verse 10) 'The Son of Man has come to seek and save the lost'. (Note that in verse 9 Jesus uses the third person rather than the second: 'He is the son of Abraham'. Jesus is now talking about Zacchaeus rather than to him). As elsewhere (Mark 2.17 par.), Jesus defends his conduct (crossing staus boundaries) by stating the purpose of his mission. His behaviour is consistent with his intention.

---

[1] The classic distinction is by Max Weber, most accessible as 'Class, Status, Party', in Weber, *From Max Weber,* ed. H. H. Garth and C. W. Mills (Oxford, New York, 1946), pp. 180-95. The concept of status has developed considerably in this century. I recommend as an introduction the following articles from the *International Encyclopaedia of the Social Sciences* (1968): 'Stratification, Social: Social Class' by Seymour M. Lipset (XV, 296-316) and 'Status, Social', by Morris Zelditch, Jr. (XV, 250-57).

[2] Karl Heinrich Rengstorf, *'Hamartolos', Theological Dictionary of the New Testament (1964), I, 320.

[3] G. Bouwman, 'La pécheresse hospitalière' (Lc. VII, 36-50), *Ephemerides Theologicae Lovanienses*[45] (1969), 179.

Jesus names as 'the lost' those whom his objectors call 'sinners' (cf. also Luke 15.6-7). The redefinition is significant. They are not sinners to be hated and driven away. They are lost, needing to be found and rejoiced over. 'Lost' implies a different status; there is something to be recovered. 'He is the son of Abraham' (v.9). He is neither a devil; nor less than human. He is a lost child of Abraham, the very criterion for membership in the community. (In the Pauline mission the equivalent criterion is replaced by the universal 'one for whom Christ died'). Jesus' mission is to locate and find those lost persons and bring them back into the community of God's people. Such restoration of the 'lost son' is described with a medical metaphor. He is 'restored to health' (hygiainein, Luke 15.27), not because he has been sick but because he is restored 'sound' socially. Likewise, mercy comes to another tax collector, who needs a 'physician', a need, however, of the healing of broken lives and broken community relationships (Matt. 9.12-12).

I omit here other groups to which Jesus extended his mission who also were hurt by their social relationships; the sick, women, children, Samaritans. But the same factors of status are present.[1]

The status boundaries that Jesus crossed are crucial to the stability of a society. That is why he provoked hostility. Status is one of the most basic elements of a social system. It is a way of controlling people. Because of it some are weak and some powerful. This inequality is socially useful. The existence of roles is inherent in being social. Roles are the way society performs its functions. They indicate how people are to behave. But the roles are highly differentiated in their meaning, Importance, and esteem. Status is a way of matching people to roles. The chaos of constantly determining anew what to expect from others is thus avoided.

When Jesus by his actions and words challenged the existing status system, he defied a major requirement for operating a social system. To those who claim that Jesus's ministry was merely personal, we reply that he could not have done anything more basic to challenge institutions and social structures. The leadership, with vested interests in maintaining society as it was structured, were threatened by his actions. They responded with enmity against him. Threats to status bring persecution. Those responsible for the threat 'come to be defined as dangerous public enemies requiring severe repressive action'.[2]

That persecution is a topic treated by most of the New Testament writings reflects in part the challenge that the Christian message and presence presented to the societies of that day. A priority for the early church was to determine if the relationships among its members would be characterized by the status distinctions of the surrounding culture. The answer was far-reaching. In the new reality made present by Jesus

---

[1] These categories often overlap. Maertens in studying twenty-seven Synoptic miracles argues that the recipient had always been excluded from Jewish identity in one degree or another (Jean-Thierry Maertens, 'La structure des recits de miracles dans les synoptiques', Studies in Religion/Sciences Religieuses 6 (1976/77), 257-58. In the story of the woman with a haemorrhage the two factors of sickness and status as a woman are particularly compounded.

[2] Jerry D. Rose, Outbreaks, The Sociology of Collective Behaviour (free, New York, 1982), pp.137, 147.

the major status distinctions of the culture—slavery, nationality, and sex—were considered null and void (Gal. 3.28). When Paul argues in Romans that the Gentiles (who according to Ephesians had no rights in the commonwealth of Israel) have been made participants in God's community through his righteousness (or 'justice' *dikaiosyne*) not by 'works'—a category of status—but by faith, he draws upon the biblical sense of justice which involves bringing people back into community.

Although social conduct in the Christian community is directly derived from the new statement about status (Col. 3.9-16), the new ideal relates to the religious basis of status (by faith, in Christ). Some have argued, as a result, that the early church did not touch the secular status systems. But any system of stratification requires a system of belief to justify and propagate the inequalities and persuade people to accept them as legitimate.[1] In a traditional society religion provides the ideological basis for status in a system. When this base is removed, the whole system is shaken.

d. The Relevance of the Principalities and Powers

The final crucial element for the social framework of the New Testament is the concept of the principalities and powers which I have developed elsewhere.[2] These powers, which are treated primarily in the Pauline letters, are angelic powers. After having been given authority by God over creation, including its social and political life, they rebelled against God and produced oppression in place of providential care. Christ has defeated these powers and carried them captive (Col. 2.15). The Pauline texts belong to a particular tradition, consisting of at least seven apocalyptic texts, which deal with God's defeat of the angelic powers. In all the texts the defeat is presented as an act of justice 'in behalf of the oppressed and against their oppressors'.[3]

With this development in Pauline thought, concern expressed in the Old Testament to resist oppressive forces in the Hebrew communities has not been abandoned. Instead it has been universalized. The oppressive forces belong to the very structure of the human community as a whole. The way is opened for both analysis and liberation to take place on a more pervasive, systemic, and universal basis.

A final note. The government to which Jesus related his ministry was not the Roman government but the local oligarchy in whose hands the Romans delegated most matters of a political nature. Noting Jesus' infrequent references to the Roman government and assuming it to be the only political body, critics have accused him of exercising an apolitical ministry. But government in his day was composed of the chief priests, the elders, and the Sanhedrin, increasingly penetrated by the Pharisees. Much of Jesus' preaching was directed against this latter group. It was they, according to the Gospels, who handed him over to death. Against *this* background, the political dimension of Jesus' ministry can be recognized as fundamental.

[1] Lipset, 'Stratification', p.305.
[2] Mott, *Biblical Ethics*, ch.1.
[3] George W. E. Nickelsburg, 'Apocalyptic and Myth in 1 Enoch 6-11'. *Journal of Biblical Literature* 96 (1977), 391-93.

2. HOW IS THE NEW TESTAMENT RELEVANT FOR SOCIAL ETHICS?

(a) The Difficulties

The second objection to the use of the New Testament for social ethics questions whether it contains the right type of material for ethics. The diverse persons raising this objection present two contrasting views of ethics. The first sees social ethics providing the correct solutions to issues faced in societies today. It is then noted that neither Jesus nor the New Testament writers provide a social programme. The New Testament lacks sufficient concreteness.

The other type of objector, in contrast, is bothered by the concreteness of the New Testament. Behind the problems raised, specific concerns are apparent. Some are concerned, for example, that Christians, whom they view as 'perfectionistic', attempt to apply directly to society such commands of Jesus as turn the other cheek, or sell one's property and give to the poor. Others[1] are concerned about the use conservative Christians make of traditional material, such as women keeping silent in the churches or slaves being obedient to their masters. Such commands from the *Haustafeln* (tables of household duties) found in Epistles are said to be 'morally irrelevant or perverse' according to an allegedly modern viewpoint. They show the flaw in believing that the Bible contains revealed morality.[2]

We are faced with the problem of specific texts and situations. The materials presented in the first part of this essay militate against understanding the New Testament as a socially conservative document. However, the general structure, principles, and missionary thrust of the New Testament which are socially critical, must be compared with concrete injunctions which seem to belie them. It is also necessary to indicate how the generalizing tendency of New Testament social thought creates concrete contemporary solutions and programmes. These two difficult tasks can be accomplished, firstly by understanding the place of concrete decision-making within the different aspects of ethical thought and, secondly by showing how principles and concrete injunctions relate in New Testament ethics.

One of the most valuable characteristics of Birch and Rasmussen's study. *Bible and Ethics in the Christian Life,* is their presentation of the diversity of ethics and the varied ways in which the writings of Scripture take up the subject. Recent writings emphasize the need to pay attention to the varied aspects of ethics.[3] Ethics includes much more than ethical decision-making or specific prescriptions. James Gustafson notes that a moral reformer of society would need to make a moral assessment of current practice, find a way to motivate people to act on the issues at stake, and state the aims of social reform.[4]

---

1 *Cf.* Christopher Hitchens, Review of *The Politics of God's Funeral,* by Michael Harrington, *In These Times* (November 16-22, 1983), 27.

2 S. Hauerwas, 'The Moral Authority of Scripture: The Politics and Ethics of Remembering', in Hauerwas, *A Community of Character* (Notre Dame, 1981), p.58.

3 Bruce C. Birch and Larry L. Rasmussen, *Bible and Ethics in the Christian Life* (Augsburg, Minneapolis, 1976). Others who emphasize the multiple aspects include Brevard Childs, Charles Curran, James Gustafson, and David Kelsey.

4 James M. Gustafson, 'From Scripture to Social Policy and Social Action', *Andover Newton Quarterly* 9 (1969), 164-67.

Beyond mere decision-making, social ethics demands that we understand the basic directions of our responsibility in society. Many of the writers struggling with the question of how the Bible relates to social ethics have stressed certain characteristics which help to define the aims of social reform. A picture of what society is meant to be comes from values associated with the new social order breaking into history. Guidelines for the basic goals, list of priorities, and basic concerns of social life come from the Bible's view of justice, inclusiveness in the membership of the new community and the new dimensions of social relationships given by sharing the participation. The New Testament thus indicates areas which ethics must consider. It is significant that the New Testament does not only spell out social aims, but also justifies them.[1] It contributes not merely to ethics but also to the theology of ethics.

This same vision provides a basis for giving a moral assessment of those directions in present social life which counter and hinder it.

(b) Motivation and the Formation of Character in Ethics

The New Testament's most unique contribution lies in the area of motivation for social reform. Herein lies the formation of character as a component of ethics. The New Testament ethic is an ethic of response to God's grace in Christ.[2] We are gracious because we have received grace. We love because we have been loved. The response is one of gratitude and also of empowerment. The love which forms our new identity also flows to correspond to those acts of God upon which our lives are founded.

This New Testament contribution to ethics does not mark a qualitative change from the Old Testament, as the latter's ethic is also a response to the mighty acts of God. The difference is a matter of intensity. The act of God is now God incarnated in history and God's own self sacrificed. Further the Spirit of God is present in those who become part of the new social existence being created, empowering and making that life possible. In the concern, in moral social reform, to move from things as they are to things as they might be, the New Testament makes an essential contribution at the level of identity, characteristic attitudes and dispositions, and fundamental interests.[3]

The New Testament's unique contribution to ethics in the areas of character and motivation does not exclude contributions to the *content* of our social obligations. For the gift of love which motivates and shapes character is part of the coming of the Reign of God. There is a strong interdependence between content and motivation.[4]

---

[1] Cf. Robert J. Daly, 'Toward a Christian Biblical Ethic', in *Critical History and Biblical Faith,* ed. T. Ryan (College Theology Society, College Theology Society Annual Publication Series, Villanova, P.A., 1979), p.214.

[2] Cf. Mott, *Biblical Ethics,* ch.2. The biblical theology of social involvement is indeed a theology of grace (cf. Pt.1 of this book).

[3] J. Gerald Janzen, 'The Bible and Our Social Institutions. A Theoretical Perspective', *Interpretation* 27 (1973), 341; cf. Charles E. Curran, 'Dialogue with the Scriptures: The Role and Function of the Scriptures in Moral Theology', in Curran, *Catholic Moral Theology in Dialogue* (Notre Dame, IN:U. of Notre Dame, 1972), p.64.

[4] Schnackenburg, 'Neutestamentliche Ethik', p.204.

(c) The Perception of Reality

The third area of ethics to which the New Testament contributes is that of the perception of reality. The content of social ethics does not only include the basic objectives and loyalties regarding social life that correspond to the aims and character that we have just discussed. There is also the way the world is perceived. Alan Geyer writes:

> Ethics is not simply an argument about what *ought* to be: it is an almost uninterrupted argument about what *is*, what *has been*, and what *will be*. The facility of public policy is often more problematical than the choices of ethical principles. Whose reading of history, which theory of human nature, which social analysis, whose worldview, which intelligence data shall we choose as being empirically sound? . . . Perception, as well as choice, is at the heart of political ethics.[1]

Perception, in part, is an aspect of character. This understanding has been correctly stressed in recent Christian social movements. Our basic attitudes and dispositions influence how we interpret both social reality and Scripture itself. When Christian character is soundly formed, listening to Scripture in the church will produce sensitivity to peoples' needs and an impatience with injustice. This disposition will lead a Christian to identify with the struggles of the oppressed in our world. In turn, Scripture will be understood at that deeper level made possible only by experiencing forgiveness and identifying with the oppressed. Otherwise, the Scriptural material dealing with these matters will be neglected.

(d) Elements of a Social Ethic in the New Testament

Ethical decisions draw upon a particular view of the world as it relates to human beings' relationship to society. Scripture's most important contribution to ethics may be the content it provides for one's worldview. In any society for there to be a genuine social ethic, certain components need to be present. People understand each of the components in a wide variety of ways; the Bible provides substantial materials for many of them. The argument[2] for using Scripture in this way for ethics is that, where normative Scriptural materials relate to the formal components of social ethics, they must be drawn upon in an authoritative manner. Although I have not seen this use of Scripture spelled out clearly,[3] I believe it is the most common form among Christian ethicists. (I have not chosen in this essay to discuss the limitations of the New Testament for ethics. It should be noted,

---

[1] Alan Geyer, 'Toward an Ecumenical Political Ethics: A Marginal American View', in *Perspectives on Political Ethics*, ed. K. Srisang (WCC, Geneva, 1983), p.135.

[2] Verhey, drawing upon the work of David Kelsey *(The Uses od Scripture in Recent Theology (Fortress, Philadelphia, 1975)), demonstrates the need to argue formally the warrants for the* particular way one is using the authority of Scripture for ethics (cf. 'The Use of Scripture in Moral Discourse', pp.217-18).

[3] Janzen does speak of the Bible's contribution in laying bare 'the enduring dynamics of human existence' (The Bible and Our Social Institutions', p.336). C. Freeman Sleeper argued that the Bible's greatest contribution to ethical thought was in the meaning it provided to contemporary secular images, 'models' in the social sciences, and categories of ethical theory ('Ethics as a Context for Biblical Interpretation', *Interpretation* 22 (1968), 451).

however, that in the formation of one's view of life, a great deal of post-biblical information and reflection is needed, including material from church history and the social sciences. These limits have been frequently discussed. As Charles Curran puts it, biblical ethics are not synonymous with Christian ethics).[1]

The Bible contributes substantial content to the following structural components of a social ethic among others: justice, the nature of humanity, the concept of history, the nature of society and groups, the understanding of power and property, and the purpose of government. The New Testament contributes more to some of these concepts than to others. In some cases it may serve primarily to show that this is a continuation of a particular perspective in the new age of grace. There are, however, additional components of social analysis to which the Bible makes little direct contribution. One example is that of middle principles. They are general patterns of social life which hold good only in certain spheres of society at a given place and time. An example would be structural unemployment in late capitalism.[2]

For justice[3] the New Testament continues the Old Testament sense of meeting basic needs and bringing marginal people into community. It adds a more inclusive understanding of status. Human nature[4] is given in the New Testament further confirmation of its creative potential as well as its propensity toward evil. Universal love through command and Christ's atonement deepens the dignity of the human being. An ethical realism is brought to the understanding of social reality while the New Testament continues the sense of individual dependency upon social life and the need for human groups. The saving events of Christ continue the meaning of history as the sphere in which humanity is liberated. The heightened expectation of the future gives urgency to the present in light of its high demands while the promise of relief for the suffering provides a critique of the conditions of the present political realm.[5]

Allowing the Bible to speak to relevant categories of social ethics enables more of its thought to be applied to a particular question than if one simply discussed the relevance of that scriptural injunction which seems to be most approximate. However, the many concrete commands of the New Testament remain. How, then, do they apply?

---

[1] Curran, 'Dialogue with the Scriptures', pp.38-39.

[2] Cf. K. Mannheim, *Man and Society in an Age of Reconstruction: Studies in Modern Social Structure* (Kegan Paul, London, 1940), Pt. IV, Sections 4-6, esp. pp.166-90.

[3] Cf. Geyer, 'Toward an Ecumenical Political Ethics', p.136.

[4] Cf. Josef Blank, 'Zum Problem "ethischer Normen" im Neuen Testament', in Blank, *Schriftauslegung in Theorie und Praxis* (Kosel, Biblische Handbibliothek 5, Munchen, 1969), p.131.

[5] Cf. Gerd Petzke, 'der historische Jesus in der sozialethischen Diskussion, Mk. 12, 13-17 par', in *Jesus Christus in Historie und Theologie*, H. Conzelmann Fest., ed. G. Strecher (Tubingen: Mohr, 1975), p.234; J. Moltmann, 'Toward a Political Hermeneutics of the Gospel', *Union Seminary Quarterly Review* 23 (1968), 313-14.

(e) The Question of Specific Commands

The different ways in which Scripture is used as an authority for morality often reflect different understandings of its nature.[1] These understandings however, are not mutually exclusive. Scripture's contribution to ethics is found in the mighty acts of God, in prevailing principles, and in theological affirmations. God also speaks authoritatively to us through particular injunctions. Transcendent truth is revealed in the Bible in diverse ways for human beings' salvation and conduct. God wills a morality for humanity ('your will be done on earth as in heaven'), and has revealed it in part through particular commands of Scripture ('he has shown you, O man, what is good'). The Scriptures, because of their place in the history of salvation, are to be understood as God speaking not only to the people of an earlier time but to us also.

This much can be affirmed without making the Bible either into an ethical code or a book of systematic ethics, a fear which many students of the hermeneutics of biblical ethics possess. The transcendent ideas are addressed to concrete situations of another time. This fact affirms the importance of history but also creates difficulties in understanding both their transcendent character and their application to a different age. The problem in interpreting a particular command is not that it is inappropriate to the nature of Scripture that God's revelation takes such a concrete form. The problem, rather, is to understand the meaning for another period of that very concreteness which makes God's Word relevant to a particular moment of history. As the whole canon is inspired, no individual text can be simply set aside. Each must be interpreted as a part of the total message of Scripture.

Stanley Hauerwas' argument that Jesus did not 'have a social ethic or have implications for the social ethic but his story *is* a social ethic'[1], is influenced by his particular view of the nature of Scripture. He fears that by lifting ethical norms from Jesus' teaching Jesus' ethics will be separated from its religious base, and virtue will be cut off from its foundation in the community which hears and remembers his story. In an effort, however, to keep Jesus' ethic attached to the story that bears it, Hauerwas questions the propositional character of biblical revelation. He appears to question not the divine source of Scripture, but rather its expressing transcendent truth in verbal concepts, when he writes, 'The very idea that the Bible is revealed (or inspired) is a claim that creates more trouble than it is worth'.[3] Further, in his attempt to understand ethics as a community's spontaneous experience arising from the story, he neglects the fact that by our nature we form our view of life by reflecting abstractly upon the confused experiences of our own world. Systematic reflection upon Scripture is an essential part of forming our worldview. In the process, norms and values applicable to new areas of our social lives will be found in the story of Jesus.

When we understand the often strange and seemingly archaic concreteness of Scripture as an historical expression of transcendental

---

[1] Cf. Verhey, 'The Use of Scripture', pp.217-18.
[2] Hauerwas, 'Jesus: The Story of the Kingdom', p.40.
[3] Hauerwas, 'The Moral Authority of Scripture', p.57.

truth designed for all humanity, we can anticipate an inexhaustible richness of meaning. Through valid exegesis we may seek in the particulars truths of greater universality. Ethical principles lie behind specific injunctions.

The hundreds of separate ethical injunctions found in the Bible have overlying themes and their own ordering of significance. Scripture points to certain basic norms which summarize others. The Gospel of Matthew, when it states in its version of the double command to love that 'on these hang the whole Law and the Prophets', presents love as the key to interpret the whole Law (Matt. 22.40; cf. 7.12). Similarly, when it presents Jesus as saying that justice, mercy, and faith 'are the more important parts' of the Law, it makes a general and abstract statement (Matt. 23.23). Norms can be identified in Scripture which apply from one time to another. Nevertheless, the concrete duties of tithing to which they are compared in this passage are not set aside: 'these also you should do'. They, too, are taken seriously.

Some specific commands found in the New Testament lend themselves by their nature to a more general meaning. 'Turn the other cheek' and 'let the women be silent in the church' are both specific injunctions. They differ markedly, however in the range of activity to which they point. The latter focuses on controlling a certain activity in a specific place. The concern of the former is hardly upon a literal slap on the face. It points to a much broader range of activity. It is paradigmatic. It is a model of behaviour which the hearer is expected to recognize and apply to other areas of life. The hearer has to recognize the principle and apply it. Most of Jesus' injunctions were paradigmatic. As such they stand in contrast to many of the specific commands of the Epistles. As in his parables, Jesus' commands had a dramatic, poetic, and pictorial character. They appealed to imagination rather than used abstract propositions to stir conscience to look for the parable.[1] 'Do not blow your trumpet'. 'Take the beam out of your own eye'. Jeremias describes the form of this teaching well. Jesus, he says, does not give instructions for all spheres of life.

> Rather, his demands give symptoms of what happens when the Reign of God breaks in . . . The *basileia* (kingdom) lays claim to the whole of life. Jesus uses illustrations to demonstrate the appearance of the new life. His disciples are to apply them to every other aspect of their lives.[2]

The advantage of this form of teaching principles is that one specific indication of what the principle means becomes the starting point of the teaching process. Although exemplary, the specific injunction is to be taken seriously. In fact, the argument that, because the injunction is paradigmatic, it is not law[3] misses the paradigmatic nature of the Torah

---

[1] Cf. C. H. Dodd, *Gospel and Law. The Relation of Faith and Ethics in Early Christianity* (Columbia U., Bampton Lectures in America 3, New York, 1951), pp.54-55, 61; and Heinz Schurmann, 'Die Frage nach der Verbindlichkeit der neutestamentlichen Wertungen und Weisungen', in *Prinzipien christlicher Moral*, ed. J. Ratzinger (Johannes, Kriterien 37, Einsielden, 1975), p.22.

[2] Joachim Jeremias, *New Testament Theology* (Scribner's, New York, 1971), p.230.

[3] Schurmann, 'Die Frage nach der Verbindlichkeit', p.22.

and other ancient Near Eastern law.[1] In addition, the fact that the commands of Jesus are difficult to obey or enforce does not rule out their character as law. Law has an important symbolic and educative function even when it does not actually control behaviour. It gives expression to social imagination, which consists of collective aspirations, visions of a future society and political hopes.[2] Yet since the controlling factor is the principle of which the injunction is an example, it allows a flexible adaptation to new historical conditions. Accordingly, Luke presents Jesus in a new situation at the end of his ministry changing the missionary instructions given earlier (Luke 22.35-38).[3]

In one other respect Jesus' concrete commands differ from many of the concrete commands of the Epistles. It is often argued that the problem with Jesus' commands is that they are too hard for this age; whilst the problem with many of the specific injunctions of the Epistles is that they seem to affirm too much the ways of the old age. The more principial are the ones pointing to the new social existence breaking into history. A tension occurs between the principle and concrete injunctions. When the tension becomes a conscious conflict, as in the story of the plucking of the ears in the grainfield, the principle prevails. Mercy replaces the duties of sabbath observance and the prohibition of consuming the priests' holy bread (Matt. 12.7). Such tension is also found within the Pauline teaching. On the one hand, there is the principle of neither male nor female, bond nor free (Gal. 3.28) pointing to a totally new definition of human relationships. On the other hand, in the *Haustafeln* there are counsels of submission.

f. The Tension between the Old and the New in New Testament Ethics

We may speak of two types of ethical teaching in Scripture. The first is that which creates radically new social relationships. The second type shows that God wills responsible conduct while the old remains.[4] Much of the tension between the two is not worked out within the canon. In the case of slavery it was not resolved for nineteen hundred years; in the case of women it now is being resolved. The first type will prevail over the second as believers become conscious of the tension between the two and begin to understand that the first is a more comprehensive statement of the meaning of the second.

[1] G. R. Driver and John C. Miles, *The Babylonian Laws* (Oxford, *Ancient Codes and Laws of the Near East*, London, 1952-55) Vol. 1, p.45; Bernard S. Jackson, *Essays in Jewish and Comparative Legal History* (Brill, Studies in Judaism in Late Antiquity 10, Leiden, 1975), pp.16, 27; Douglas Start, 'The Law(s)—Covenant Stipulations for Israel', in Gordon D. Fee and Douglas Stuart, *How to Read the Bible for All Its Worth* (Zondervan, Grand Rapids, MI, 1981), pp.140-41, 143.

[2] Guy Rocher, 'Le Droit et l'imaginaire social', *Recherches Sociographiques* 23 (1982), pp.65-74.

[3] Cf. David L. Dungan, *The Sayings of Jesus in the Churches of Paul. The Use of the Synoptic Tradition in the Regulation of Early Church Life* (Fortress, Philadelphia, 1971), pp.72-73.

[4] Krister Stendahl speaks of the tension between the new and the old and how Paul in 1 Corinthians had to defend the old against those who overstated the new while in Galatians he strongly stated the new against those who defended the old *(The Bible and the Role of Women. A Case Study in Hermeneutics* (Fortress, Facet Books Biblical Series 15, Philadelphia, 1966), pp.35-37; cf. Donald R. Wilson, in Peter DeJong and Donald R. Wilson, *Husband and Wife, The Sexes in Scripture and Society* (Zondervan, Grand Rapids, MI, 1979), pp.260, 344-45.

g. The Appeal to Creation

Colossians presents the abolishing of false distinctions among human beings as a renewal of the situation at the creation: 'Do not be false to each other . . . by putting on the new nature which is being renewed in knowledge according to the image of its creator, where there is neither Greek nor Jew . . .' (Col. 3.9-11). Jesus' appeal to the time of creation—'from the beginning it was not so'—in dealing with the divorce question equally is significant (Matt. 19.4-8; Mark 10.4-8).

The importance of the appeal to creation can be shown by reference to Ernst Troeltsch's distinction between absolute and relative natural law. Natural law reflects the conviction that moral obligation should correspond to the nature of the world as God created and maintained it. *Absolute* natural law reflects the creation as God intended it to be and as it was in the beginning. Social life is characterized by equality and harmonious relationships. *Relative* natural law takes into account the fall into sin and the contingencies of society. There is an acceptance of institutional relationships which are less than ideal but which serve to keep a check on sin. Either absolute natural law can be dismissed as no longer relevant or the distinction between absolute and relative natural law can be minimalized. In either case there is an acceptance of things as they are and a pessimism regarding change. When the two types of natural law are differentiated and maintained, however, the appeal to absolute natural law can be the basis of social criticism.[1]

By drawing normatively upon the original state, Jesus shows that these ideal standards continue current beyond the fall. God's Reign breaking into history is restoring lost creation. In his appeal, Jesus raises a powerful and radical critique. Like the relative natural law, the arrangements of the Mosaic divorce provisions are not adequate. David Dungan shows how Jesus changed the Pharisees' wording from 'What did Moses *command*', to 'Moses *permitted*' (Matt. 19.7-8).[2] Relative natural law likewise deals not with behaviour commanded, but permitted because of sin.[3]

We may say that in New Testament ethics concrete commands reflect the need to control[4] behaviour in areas not transformed by the higher demand. They are, however, in tension with the demands of creation reiterated in the new order. Thus the absolute natural law remains available in its critical function. Furthermore, it is not the concessionary materials but the demands of God's Reign, which has come with Christ, which constitute the prophetic word which still corrects the moral levels of the church and the world.

[1] Troeltsch, *Social Teachings*, Vol. 1, pp.260, 344-45.

[2] Dungan, *Sayings of Jesus*, p.121.

[3] See also David Daube, 'Concessions to Sinfulness in Jewish Law', *Journal of Jewish Studies*, 10 (1959), pp.11-12. Daube uses the terminology *ius naturale and ius civile* rather than our distinction of absolute and relative natural law.

[4] O. M. .T. O'Donovan follows Thomas Aquinas and the Reformers in seeing Moses' concession in the divorce ordinance as reflecting the social and political function of laws (in contrast to their moral and educational purpose) of controlling what cannot be eradicated ('Toward an Interpretation of Biblical Ethics', *Tyndale Bulletin* 27 (1976), p.66).

3. NEW TESTAMENT SOCIAL THOUGHT AND THE PRESENT
a. The Historical Gap

Many writers have raised a concern about particular commands, because they believe them to be tied so closely to the first century that they have little value for our situation today.

There are important constants as well as differences between biblical times and our own. Hiers argues that the teachings of Jesus are valid for us on the grounds that neither God's nature nor that of humankind has changed substantially.[1] Conflicts over power and the oppression of the weak by the strong recur in history. In dealing with such situations one can apply the abiding word of God.

In dealing with the concrete particulars, one must comprehend how they function in the community. Those who want to apply biblical injunctions literally to contemporary societies fail to examine their function in the original community. As a result they do not recognize that the function may be carried out differently in another culture.

We must note what past and present societies have in common and where they differ. When this is not done, a particular injunction may be applied to matters which, despite contrary appearances, are different. As a result the Word of God is misused. The Word of God to one church may be that women are not to usurp authority by teaching heresy (1 Tim. 2.11-12).[2] That Word will apply to them or to a different group if the same problem of heresy is posed in another situation; not, however, where heresy is not the issue in the same way.

Limits imposed on direct injunctions are not only due to the vast diversity of human culture. The Holy Spirit creates a new consciousness which makes some injunctions no longer necessary. When the meaning of 'love your neighbour as yourself' and 'there is neither slave nor free' is more fully comprehended, the command for slaves to obey their masters becomes inapplicable, because slavery itself has been condemned before the Word of God and abolished.

The argument that the New Testament ethics are inapplicable because they presuppose a view of history unacceptable to the modern world is a different kind of objection. It touches on the very structure of New Testament thought. The thesis of Jack Sanders' book, *Ethics in the New Testament*, is that New Testament ethics depend on the expectation of the end and are meaningless outside this context. Jesus' hard sayings about taking no thought about tomorrow are capable of obedience only by taking seriously Jesus' expectations that the end of history, was imminent. We, however, live in a time 'that knows it does not stand before God's imminent coming' (p.64).

Two basic problems in Sanders' argument prevent the contemporary Christian getting off the hook so easily. The first is that he

---

[1] Hiers, *Jesus and Ethics*, p.149.
[2] Cf. David M. Scholer, 'Exegesis: 1 Timothy 2.18-15', *Daughters of Sarah* 1,4 (May 1975), p.7-8.

misrepresents the essence of New Testament eschatology. The mark of the New Testament's view of history is not the expectation of an immediate end but the tension which exists between those aspects of the end time which have already come and those which are soon to come. Thus a further delay did not contradict the expectation. At a later date others could experience, as did the early church, the same tension of the already and the not yet.

The tension allows both time and the created world to continue. The demand posed by Jesus in his proclamation of the Reign was not totally new but summed up the values associated with the centuries old Hebrew expectation. The Reign was a renewal of God's creative intention. Jesus' ethics therefore, are a call to live according to the way things were created. They are not outrageous and inapplicable demands which only make sense within one strange view of history. In his most demanding teaching, Jesus appealed to God's providence over creation in calling his disciples to trust him fully for the essentials of life (Matt. 6.30; Luke 12.28) or to love their enemies (Matt. 5.45). The common element behind Jesus' appeals is his faith in God the Creator and Redeemer who is bringing about a new Reign.[1]

The second problem in Saunders' argument is that he neglects the number of contemporary Christians for whom the imminence of Christ's return plays an important part in their consciousness. The growing threat of nuclear holocaust has heightened the relevance of these convictions to the present. The expectation of the end as a context for New Testament ethics is no problem for those who live with the hope that Christ will return in their lifetime. The urgency which Christ imparted to his disciples and which motivated them to carry out God's mission was to be that of every succeeding generation.

Yet we live twenty centuries after that proclamation of God's coming was made. Certainly, the stewardship of justice and God's creation requires entertaining the possibility that ours is not the generation which 'will not pass before all these things are fulfilled'. The first century expectation of the end was not incompatible, however, with a sense of responsibility for the future. Paul, in a passage in which he is acutely aware of the end of the age, gives counsel regarding marriage on the basis of how the godliness of the children will be affected (1 Cor. 7.14).[2]

b. A Christian Ethic for a Non-Christian Society?

Finally, there is the problem of the relationship between faith and an ethic for society. In terms of the categories developed in this essay, since the formation of character is a major component of ethics, since it is the most unique contribution of New Testament ethics and since it takes place in the church, how can the ethic apply to those outside?

[1] Cf. H. R. Niebuhr, *Christ and Culture*, p.22.
[2] Dungan, *Sayings of Jesus*, p.120; cf. pp.117, 119, 133. Cf. W. D. Davies, 'The Relevance of the Moral Teachings of the Early Church', in *Neotestamentica et Semitica*, M. Black Fest., ed. E. E. Ellis and M. Wilcox (Clark, Edinburgh, 1969), pp.36-38.